Catching the Waves

Catching the Waves

A Collection of Poems About Love, Life,
Friendships & Everything In Between.

Monika Bardhan

PARTRIDGE
A Penguin Random House Company

ISBN: Softcover   978-1-4828-2632-6
               eBook   978-1-4828-2633-3

To order additional copies of this book, contact
Toll Free 800 101 2657 (Singapore)
Toll Free 1 800 81 7340 (Malaysia)
orders.singapore@partridgepublishing.com

www.partridgepublishing.com/singapore

Contents

Dedication

This book is dedicated in the loving memory of my beloved maternal grandparents,
Upendra Chandra Das (1903 – 1979) & Usha Rani Das (1917 – 2009), for being my lifelong inspirational icons & the coolest grandparents ever!

&

Also dedicated to my loving family for their endless love & support in everything I do, & for putting up with me on a daily basis with lots of love ☺

xoxox

Preface

It has always been my dream to publish my book of poems, which I have personally composed. It all began when I was nine years old, and since then, I have been writing about everything and everyone that has touched my life and influenced me in so many ways.

The most noted influence was my wonderful late maternal grandfather, Mr. Upendra Chandra Das, who passed away in 1979. He wrote the first piece of this book entitled "The Indian Milkmaid in Malaysia", which so eloquently describes what the life of a milkmaid was like in this country way back in late 1960s. I included his poem in this book as a tribute to the amazing man who clearly changed my life forever.

The poem "Love and Care for Older Parents" is a beautiful poignant piece written by my amazing mother, Arati Bardhan. Being one of the biggest influences in my life, her profound words touched a deep cord inside me, which made me appreciate my parents even more, and made me grateful that they have instilled good values in their three children.

In February 1993, my dearest sister, Nita Bardhan, presented me with a lovely journal on my birthday where I could write all my poems. Hence, Catching The Waves tells many different stories in the form of poetry, which is all about love, life, friendships and everything in between.

From politics, world events, family and friendships, to sacrifices, sorrow, triumphs and tragedy, this book encompasses every aspect of human nature and everything that occurs in our daily lives.

I sincerely hope that you will enjoy reading these unique pieces immensely as much as I did writing them.

Monika Bardhan ☺

Acknowledgements

My heartfelt and deepest thanks to:

My late maternal grandfather, Upendra Chandra Das – for inspiring me to write, and for being my true inspiration to be the best poet that I could be. I love you and miss you very much always and forever.

My late maternal grandmother, Usha Rani Das – for teaching me to love unconditionally, and appreciate the simple things in life. You are dearly missed and loved everyday.

Dilip Kumar Bardhan – a good father and husband. Thank for your love and support, providing the best for your family, and for being there for us all over the years.

Arathi Bardhan – for being the best mother & best friend ever. You truly inspire me to be a better person everyday. Your unconditional love and unwavering support is always there to carry me through my days. You are truly a woman of great substance, and I love you forever more, Ma.

Nita Bardhan – my sweetest and coolest sister! Thank you for all your love and support, and for always being there for me no matter what. You make everyday so much fun and joyful. You are my wonderful best friend forever, and I love you very much always.

Papia, Randy, Robin & Alina Ly – my family away from home. Thank you for your love & support over the years. It is very much appreciated.

Sandeep Ray – my childhood best friend & my knight in shining armor! You have always been there for me through good times and bad, and I cherish our wonderful, warm & loving friendship that has lasted four decades. Hugs & cheers!

Hans Wilhelm Andersson – my right arm, my best friend, my saving grace & the joy of my heart always. Thank you for your immense love, encouragement, inspiration & support. Thank you for always being there & for always believing in me, no matter what. Love you lots. You rock!

And, lastly, to all the important people in my life and my extended family, for all your immense love, support and wonderful everlasting friendship – Vinod Shankar Nair, Fahim Fazli, Shanthi Ratnam, Siva Govindaraju & Jevan Gunaselan.

Indian Milkmaid In Malaysia

Written by my late maternal grandfather, Mr. Upendra Chandra Das, circa 1969.

Half a dozen cows she had, heifers and calves a few
Smiling and talking, though very old, betel nuts she would chew.
Morn till night she would work, and walk on the road
Selling her milk from door to door, on her head the load.
Bottles of milk in a wicker basket set nicely in balance
Both her hands swinging at sides, away she would dance.
"A rotten son I have got, looks after pleasures of self
Old and weak though I am, he never cares to help".
With winds she would speak about her son for a while
"What are you speaking of?" if asked, she would simply smile.
A few months later, she went to India with her rotten child
Got him married to a longhaired bride – lovely, beautiful and mild.
Happy she was for a few months, and then she had an attack of cholera
In her holy land, she breathed her last, the final scene of an opera.

Ode To A Samaritan

Dedicated in Loving & Respected Memory of Mr. Karpal Singh (1940-2014)
-    Father-figure, Mentor, Loyal friend, Human Rights Activist &
     Politician.

The day dawned so clear and bright,
The morning dew being filtered by the rays of sunlight.
But a nagging feeling persisted throughout the day,
Refusing to budge or just simply go away.
Then came the shattering news like the strike of a thunder bolt,
Leaving us shocked and speechless, feeling so totally lost.
The tears of grief kept flowing, our hearts bleeding in sorrow,
Unable to believe that we'll never, ever, meet again tomorrow.
As realization sets in and we contemplate at fate,
We still can't accept the fact that you're gone, the pain is too great.
Your healing touch, sense of humour and gentle smile,
Made everyone's troubles disappear, even just for a while.
Never a person to let the worst situations get you down,
You brought life, happiness and laughter to all those around.
Your words of wisdom; your courage and determination
Will always be treasured like gold, as will be your dedication.
The depth of this enormous loss and sadness only few will comprehend,
For this is not farewell but a tribute to you – our amazing mentor,
beloved father and dearest friend.

17.4.2014

Mama Mia – Arati

The origin of a child is that of the mother,
Who is, by far, the best human being amongst others.
She is the one who gave me life all those years ago,
Nurturing and carrying me inside with love and tenderness so.
From the time I was born, her adoration knew no bounds
Cherishing and protecting me from the bad and ugly around.
Through the years she watched me grow and prosper,
From observing me take the first step right up to hanging my diaper!
Her serenity and inner strength embraces me like a glove,
Her pure beauty and gentle heart giving her total love.
Through her difficult childhood she has experienced so much,
The hardships in life she encountered has given her that special touch.
Her unique way with people has made her one of a kind,
Her courage and great determination making her a rare find.
The lessons in life that she's taught me is of immense value,
Making me love and respect her with greater depth and virtue.
The sacrifices she's made for me to get the best in life,
Portrays her to be a fantastic mother, career woman and a wife.
She has so much to offer, both in personality and in presence,
Which makes her, sincerely, a true woman of substance.

20.9.1994

Father Knows Best (For Baba)

So alike yet so different we both are,
Yet to me you're like a bright shining star.
You watched me grow and changed my diaper,
You watched me take my first step up a ladder.
I was like a hurricane running all around,
Driving you up the wall when I was never found!
As I grew up, you taught me to live my life,
To work hard, to achieve the best, to strife.
The lessons I learnt from you are so rare,
The sacrifices you made show how much you care.
Though you never show your feelings so clearly,
Your love and support is reflected in your actions so freely.
I have disobeyed you countless of times,
Yet you took it with a stride and never seemed to mind.
We have argued about so many silly things,
Yet you respected my opinion about everything.
Even at this age II still need you by my side,
I can confide in you for I have nothing to hide.
I feel so fortunate that I have you as a father,
For you, so precious and unique like no other!

6.12.1995

Flesh And Blood

Family is one thing that will never go away,
They will always stick by you come what may.
Like the saying goes, "Blood is Thicker than Water",
You are always there every time for one another.
They are such a comfort when things aren't going right,
They help to keep your perspective in direct light.
Even if you've done something that seems like a crime,
They will scold you then and forgive you in a short time.
Friends may come and go in and out of your life,
Your father always faithful to his ever loving wife.
Your brothers and sisters will argue till no end,
But always remember your family is your best friend.
You might have a difference of opinion every now and then,
But your family sticks by you no matter when.
As you grow older, you'll appreciate them more,
Your love and respect for each other remains intact as before.
You may change for the better or for worse,
You will share happiness and a major bowl of tears.
If there is ever a catastrophe like a major flood
Your family will always be your flesh and blood.

9.11.1995

My Sweet Sister & Bff - Nita

If I search the entire world high and low
I'd never be able to find a better sister somehow.
Someone I consider to be the best friend ever
For we have stuck through good and bad times together.
You have always been there for me through the days
Just like I'll be there for you today and always.
The day you fell ill was too powerful to bear
I prayed for your speedy recovery, wished I was with you then and there.
The waiting was agonizing, to hear you were well
I'm so glad you're feeling better because that's really swell!
I would never bear to lose you or the rest of the family
For you are the centre of my universe and mean a great deal to me.
What in the world would I do without a gem like you?
Despite the fact you drive me up the wall through and through!
The closeness that we share is precious like a rare stone
The love and loyalty between us goes deep to the bone.
I'm so happy that things are finally going your way
May you be blessed with good fortune on every other day.
I can only say these words which come straight from my heart
We will always be sisters and best friends whether near or far apart.

2.2.1996

Pretty Pia

It is now ten o'clock, not so late in the night
My thoughts straying towards the past ever so slight.
The years have gone by so very rapidly
It seems like I just saw yesterday and you seem so happy.
Has it been five years since we last met?
Though I know it was January 1991 to the last date.
We have both changed since we last saw each other
We are so different though we are sisters.
The fights we had as children play in my mind
The fond memories I have of you not far behind.
I miss you & I think about you all the time
You are my dearest friend worth every little dime.
You are a mother now, still so young and sweet
You are still the same mischievous girl, never missing a beat!
Even though we hardly ever keep in touch
The love and affection between us still ever strong as much.
I am counting the days until I can see you again
As I see the sunshine and the fall of drops of rain.
Whatever you do in life, I back you up one hundred percent
For you are my dearest sister who is a gift that is God sent.

2.2.1996

Dadubhai, Our Angel In Heaven

Looking back at the days that have gone by
It's amazing how fast time can sometimes fly.
Just seems like yesterday that I was this little girl
Who sat on your lap with pigtails and natural curls.
You were so handsome and had a powerful zest for life
Telling wonderful tales and smiling tenderly at your dear wife.
Remembering the fun times spent at the Tanjung Kling House
Away from my mum's prying eyes, scurrying around like a mouse!
You let me be free and left me to do as I pleased
Without a care in the world, you made me feel totally at ease.
You are a man full of wisdom, a gentleman full of grace
Full of courage and passion,, that is etched in every line on your face.
Your unwavering love and total devotion to dearest Lily
Your wicked sense of humour that made her laugh silly!
Would always put everyone in a good mood and be happy
No matter how bad the situations were, even for the weary.
You are still here, your soothing presence felt every night & every day
Your gentle soul always keeping the sadness at bay
You will always be the greatest hero, the shining knight among all men
For you, my darling Dadubhai, will always be that special shining star
like an angel in heaven.

5.7.2005

Insecurious Child

You are at a point in your life right now
Where everything seems so confusing somehow.
You're feeling so lost in your own world
As you become a woman from a young girl.
The last few months have been a burden
Everything happening at once, all of a sudden.
You thought that you had made new friends
But they turned out to be enemies in the end.
The disappointments that you have had to face
Are all part of the current difficult phase.
The insecurities that you have tucked inside
Reflects all the secrets and feelings that you hide.
Still ever the curious child that you always were
You're still searching for that something out there.
Because you fell in love with the right man at the wrong time
Your family doesn't give a damn about you and think you're not worth
a dime.
But to the four of us, you're really a treasure
The time spent with you is always a pleasure.
Regardless of the fact that you drive me up the wall
I will always love you and catch you when you fall.

6.12.1995

The Other Woman

She lurks about in the periphery of his life
She can never take the place of his lawfully wedded wife.
She brings him the love and affection she longs for
Something which he gets from his wife no more.
Their passion blazes out of control beyond their limit
The wife always turning the other cheek, pretending not to see it.
Bonded by the wows that they cannot seem to break
The love triangle existing will ultimately bring heartache.
No one will emerge the victor in this game of treason
Someone will get hurt for no rhyme or reason.
The affair will continue for many, many years to come
He will always have days at end and faithfully return home.
How much longer can this charade carry on?
When the love for his wife is long dead and gone.
How can they endure the fact that nothing is the same
With he and his woman living together in shame.
'Tis a tragedy for such an unfortunate thing to happen
When knowing that the husband has another woman.
But this is the pattern of life in which they have chosen
Even if it is a weight they carry like a great burden.

6.1.1996

Waiting In Vain

She gazes out into the distant glow of the horizon
Watching the sun come up in its glorious perfection.
The strains of the seagulls flying in the sky
The shrill cry echoing the anxiety, making her sigh.
She waits in vain for the love soon to return
Igniting the candle within her, so strong it burns.
She shades her eyes as her glance skims the ocean
Looking and hoping for some sign of recognition.
Her heart beat slows as disappointment sets in
A cloudy gloom already taking place from within.
The realization of the fact he is not coming back
Sets her off kilter, tossing her senses off track.
The sudden void in her life seems bleak and empty
Her soul laden with sorrow as she looks to the sea.
Her heart shatters into a million tiny fragments
Her mind a kaleidoscope of images and patterns
She still stands rooted to the spot, still hoping
She will continue to wait and wait without ever stopping.
Though the waiting might seem endless and in vain
She knows deep down that he will return to her again.

19.1.1996

Outside Looking In

Analysing our feelings is something we all do
When we are depressed and lonely, feeling totally blue.
This is one of the rare times when I'm experiencing the above
In desperate need for companionship, attention and love.
A zillion and one thoughts run through my active mind
Leaving all tied up in knots and in an absolute bind.
For the life of me, I can't figure out what is really wrong
To put my finger on it will probably take me all night long.
I think about the years gone by with a sudden flash of insight
The friends I've made, the loves I've lost, the darkness in the light.
When I'm with my closest pals, I feel I really belong with them
But still I feel so lost and alone, a feeling I really condemn.
It's as if I'm on the outside, a stranger looking right in
Trying to blend with everyone in the harmonious circle within.
But as hard as I try to fit in with the familiar crowd
Thy solitary seat will not permit me to express my thoughts aloud.
With a vortex of emotions swirling inside my inner self
It's hard, I know – but I have to dust clear the ancient book on the shelf.
For come tomorrow will be another bright sunny day
Full of challenges and hopes it will all have to face, come what may.

13.6.1994

Fate

There are times when one often wonders
Why we are so different compared to others.
As we weigh the pros and cons of each passing day
Not knowing what we're going to cross along the way.
Then suddenly things took an expected turn
Leaving one shocked, speechless, feeling the burn.
One minute you are feeling loved and totally at peace
Then it's all shattered like splintered glass in pieces.
How would a love so pure become so degraded
The adoration you once felt for him now seems jaded.
Mixed emotions of affection and hate stirring in a bowl
All directed at one person from deep within your soul.
You realized this was going to happen but timing was all wrong
He should have been honest for he knew the truth all along.
But whatever has happened may have been for the best
To me it seems about strength of mind – the ultimate test.
It's only a matter of time before all wounds heal
For you are strong enough to survive this unforgettable ordeal.
At least you are surrounded by family and friends whom you love
Because you are a fighter and you will make it with God's help from
above.

1.7.1994

Nothing Ever Lasts

Wishful thinking is something we daily do
Knowing what we wish for won't ever come true.
No matter how hard we try and dream
Things are not as easy as they seem.
It's hard to tell who your friends really are
The ones who are loved and dear are always so far.
Surrounded by a thousand souls wearing smiling faces
From all walks of life, coming from different places.
One can never tell who is honest or evil
Who is an angel, a saint, Satan or a devil.
A marriage may appear to be made in heaven
In some case, divorce is the ultimate weapon of separation.
Two people may have been best pals as children
Suddenly, one betrays the other and the friendship is broken.
A family may once have been happy and content
Infidelity and rebellion then sets in at the wrong moment.
A young infant is born and an old man is dead and gone
Portraying life as a vicious cycle rotating on its own.
For those who think that life is always a bed of roses
Think again, people, and strive to make the right choices.

4.10.1994

Great Going, Guns!

All your life something seemed to be missing
What was it? – that you couldn't stop wondering.
It made you restless and more determined to find out
What you were looking for without a doubt.
And then she came across your path out of the blue
Making your gloomy day suddenly bright and new.
She brought abundant rays of hope and sunshine
Into your world, which is now so full and divine.
Her sincerity and unconditional love for you only
Has made you totally whole again, never to be lonely.
With her depth, sense of humour and understanding
She has made you quit drinking and stop smoking!
Not that you committed the above sins much anyway
But she managed to heal you in her own special way.
Ah! But what wonders a woman does to a man!
Like lying in the sun for an hour and getting a tan!
But, seriously though, I'm really happy for you
To have finally found love and contentment that's so true
May you both have the success and happiness that you so richly deserve
And grow old together with this great love that lifelong you will preserve.

16.10.1994

Constellation

The stars up in heaven shining so bright
Some so tiny, almost out of sight.
They sparkle like priceless 18 karat diamonds
At times, appearing to be like small polished almonds.
They seem smaller than the glowing sun
Some of them being larger than the next one.
The stars create a design within the universe
Each one so unique, yet they seem too diverse.
Like an embryo from God, to a foetus they will grow
Into an unborn child, they will continue to glow.
From the Great Bear to the Big Dipper
From Andromeda to the sweet Seven Sisters.
The life of the stars dates back to an era before Christ
Before everything else, they were there first.
One star can explode to create many more
Some bigger and brighter than the ones before.
As astronomers research with never-ending fascination
The heavens continue to create more constellations.
That we will envision even in the next millennium
And have more wonders in store for the next generation to appreciate them.

12.9.1999

Crossroads

It's been months since I picked up a pen and paper
To write a few words that would make some meaning later.
But right now my brain seems to be a little misty
From the long drought of silence that has been so empty.
Right now I feel so out-of-sorts, a feeling I can't define
So puzzling this is when now my life should be doing fine.
I have everything in the world at this very minute
A career, loads of friends and the entire world at my feet.
At one time I was so full of energy and so full of ambition
I was so full of zest and got involved with no inhibitions.
But suddenly I find myself at a complicated intersection
Immediately at a loss with no definite sense of direction.
Right now I have some crucial decisions to make
To the point of cracking my head all night if that's what it takes.
If only I did not feel so tied up in knots deep inside
If only I did not fear and have worries I wish I could hide.
What have I got to lose when everything is going right?
Where has it gone, that secure feeling I used to hold tight?
So this brings me back to square one all over again
As I continue to rake my brain and make decisions in the rain.

7.8.1996

Forever With Love

The memories haunt her night and day
The times they spent together precious in every way.
She remembers his smile stretching from ear to ear
Wishing he were there with her, right now, right here.
They always say distance makes the heart grow fonder
It is so true because her love for him has grown stronger.
The thousands of miles seem to stretch between them so far
He is still and will forever be her bright, shining star.
The musical tones of his voice is like a soothing balm
Caressing her frazzled nerves until she is calm.
What she would give to fly him to where she is
For every time she thinks of him, her heart goes into spasm.
Every moment she is wondering what he is up to
Knowing he is thinking of her as much in the same way too.
That he still feels the passion and the desire for her
The same feelings burn strongly inside of her for only him right here.
As they still remember all the good and bad times they have shared
Fate has given them a second chance to rediscover the love they spared.
Whatever he decides or wherever in this life he may be
She will always be there to love him and support him, which she guarantees.

22.4.2007

Life In Motion

Exhaustion is something that we face in our daily lives
Feeling lethargic, yet we continue to strive.
When the mind says "no" but the body says "yes"
We still aim high to give all our very best.
Sometimes, we push ourselves beyond the limit
Slowly wearing ourselves down until it is a habit.
No matter how mentally tired we are at any time
Our physical strength will not be worth a dime.
In this world today, where ultimate success counts
Where the competition to be the best knows no bounds.
The pressure builds till it reaches the maximum peak
The race to the finish line is the end for a mind gone weak.
No one seems to realize that the body is not a mechanical source of production
It cannot go on continuously for 24 hours without relaxation.
Being exhausted all the time will do more harm than good
Taking away every sense of humour, replacing it with a bad mood.
If one is not careful, fraying tempers and depression will set in
Ruining what peace of mind we have deep within.
So, don't ever let anything run you to the ground
There is more to life than work, and there is happiness to be found.

16.9.1999

Reflections Of Life

Sitting here, thinking, watching the sun go down
About life, and the people all around.
The drastic changes that have occurred so fast
The metamorphosis towards the present from the past.
So, taking a long trip down memory lane
Reflecting on the past and present joys and pain.
The friendships that have come and gone along the way
Very few of them were meant to permanently stay.
After being together for such a long time
Realising that a few treasured souls are worth a dime.
It is hard to find people you can really trust
And not be taken for granted like an old book collecting dust.
But these things do occur and cannot be avoided
Even to the mere mortals who are so easily deluded.
The betrayals, disappointments, heartaches and torments
Are the expected things that happen at unexpected moments.
But despite the harshness of life that sometimes seems absurd
Some elements of good and happiness exist in every sense of the word.
So, cut down on expectations and take each day as it comes
Accept what life has to offer and content you will become.

15.11.1993

Food For Thought

In a world filled with so much chaos and confusion
I often wonder and dream about all nations coming together in union.
As I sit within the peaceful atmosphere right next to my Mama
Thinking about the other orphaned, hungry child in war torn Bosnia.
Wishing that I could save the millions of men, women and children dying
Who are mercilessly killed and tortured within the rumble of Rwanda who is bleeding.
All these are perfect examples of crimes against humanity
When, where, who, why and how it occurs baffles everybody.
This depicts the cruel, malicious and evil side of human nature
Making us seem like devils in disguise cloaked as angels foreseeing a bleak future.
It shows so clearly that the most malignant cancer in the world today
Are human beings who see fit to do as they please without a care.
Who seem to justify their actions through mere words, lectures and speeches
Never to realize they do not seem to practice what their fellowman preaches.
Why can't we just for once comprehend that this world is drying of its juice
And lay down our weapons, put aside our anger and declare a truce.
Why can't we realize that all the wars, killing and bloodshed is so unnecessary
And live together as one big family united with peace and harmony.
So just take a moment to ponder about all the suffering and the sorrow
And definitely make the children's dreams of yesterday become the realities of tomorrow.

2.9.1994

Silent Rain

The sound of the wind whispering through the air
Blowing in various directions with unique flair.
The sound of leaves rustling in the breeze
Filling you with contentment and totally at ease.
Without realization the perfect day turns misty
Clear blue skies become slate gray and cloudy.
Mere words cannot describe the feelings inside
The haunting beauty even nature cannot hide.
Tiny drops of water come tumbling down from the sky
So synchronized with each other, making you sigh.
Though it gains momentum with each passing second
Makes you wish that you could prolong the moment.
I look out the window as it continues to pour
Wishing for the very best and a whole lot more.
Thinking about what's in store for the next day
Praying good fortune for me, and those far away.
The dew on the leaves reflecting rays of sunlight
It's brightness taking away the fear and preventing my flight.
The continuing shower washes away the intense pain
Giving me courage and wisdom through the silent rain.

2.7.1994

Hale-Bob, The Heavenly Miracle

Gazing up into the heavens at the bright moon and stars
I see a flash of light suddenly appearing from afar.
Like a tiny white dot, followed by a long fuzzy tail
It appeared to move so slowly like an old train on a rail.
Once in a while, it would burn brighter and sparks would fly
Like a precious solitaire diamond in the darkened sky.
Its awesome beauty was utterly and intensely mesmerising
All my attention focused on it because it was totally captivating.
It wove its magic around me like a warm embracing glove
Capturing my heart so tenderly and filling it with love.
Playing tricks with my overactive mind, my imagination running wild
It was a sight to behold, turning me into a delightful child.
My eyes sparkled brilliantly as that mysterious little light
Giving me a whole new outlook at life with a sudden flash of insight.
Making me realise that life as a whole is definitely worth living
For it should not be wasted but be made to be completely fulfilling.
As I went on gazing at that unique object fleeting between the clouds
It strengthened my determination and cleared all my doubts.
Looking back for one last time, counting tonight as my lucky bet
That I got to see the once-in-a-lifetime miracle - The Hale-Bob Comet.

18.5.1997

Crimes Of War

Under the hot sun broken by violent summer showers
Kosovo is waking up to a midsummer nightmare of fires.
The Serbs being the vicious killing machine at work
The ethnic cleansing of Muslims progressing through a snake's network.
The horrors stay locked in one's vivid mind
Bits of ashen bone are all that is left behind.
Relatives pick through charred remains in their smoldering houses
Where human debris are placed in little bags, each tagged with names of children or spouses.
Chunks of roasted flesh cast a gory litter the ground
Documenting death in living colour all around.
The evidence before our own eyes is so damning
Showing the calculated nature of atrocities that is so condemning.
This is a shameful mosaic of a season of slaughter
As the city lay in silent ruin even the day after.
For it is hard to imagine all of these at once
To take in and digest all this madness at a glance.
When we are supposed to be living in a civilised world
How and why people are subjected to immense violence is yet to be a mystery revealed.
So, it is time for the politicians and the public to wake up and take notice
And determine how best to bring the guilty ones to justice.

12.7.1999

Before The Flood

Not many people know of the Three Gorges Dam
Being built along the Yangtze River where nature once swam.
China's most ambitious project since the great wall
To be completed in the year 2009 by one and all.
It will displace two million people as it swallows up cities, farms and canyons
Like erasing a child's pretty picture drawn from crayons.
Placed on a higher ground, new cities rise like forests of concrete
As the common folk watch their homes being demolished with grief and defeat.
Thirteen replacement cities built along 370 miles of flowing waterway
Rapids and whirlpools now challenge boatmen in disarray.
This is the dream of China's leaders for most of this century
That is carried into the next millennium with all its glory.
Drowned in the dam's reservoir will be the endangered Chinese River Dolphin
Who are unaware that they might parish along with their next of kin.
Unexcavated sites will be lost forever in a tomb of water and sediment
Forever burying them, along with history and sentiment.
As the dam's construction goes and the water level rises
Human resources will be depleted before anyone ever realises.
For no price tag has been attached to cultural heritage
The Three Gorges Dam has sadly made sure of that as we come of age.

15.2.1999

Almost Out Of Africa

- A tribute to the wild gorillas of the Congo.

The king of the mountains sits on his hilltop, looking majestic
Surveying his surroundings with accuracy that is so artistic.
Watching closely as his mate nurses her young ones
All the while looking out for inconspicuous poachers holding guns.
Sensitive and perceptive to each and every sound of the jungle
He hunts for food to feed his children who are playing in a tangle.
Though he may be ferocious and weigh 450 pounds
Just one look into those soulful eyes will melt your heart to the ground.
His gentleness and loving gesture so tender and mild
Throws out a lifetime of misconceptions into the African wild.
He and his clan are slowly being driven out of the Central African tent
Due to poaching and human encroachment into their natural
environment.
They are now in danger of being totally extinct
Unless we act fast, using all our resolve and instinct.
There are only 650 of the likes of DIGIT left in the world
For those endangered species are as priceless as gold.
They are the ones who keep the spirit of the wild alive
Preserving tradition, peace, and the strong will to survive.
So, contribute in whatever way to protect the mighty
Or else, they will be erased from the face of the Earth for eternity.

9.2.1999

The Sunflower House

The quaint wooden house sits in a tiny corner of Sweden called Tanum
Painted in bright yellow, it's vibrant colour taking away all the gloom.
Sitting in the middle of the forest in its majestic glory
The picture of a beautiful sunflower, so sweet and merry.
With a grassy marsh amid an amazing green meadow
The giant birch tree giving some natural privacy within its shadow.
The Sunflower House is filled with immense space & a cozy hall
Full of love and joy engraved in each and every wall.
The home is well insulated to preserve the coolness in the summer heat
And then it generates soothing warmth that even a cold winter cannot beat.
The owner of the house is Hans Wilhelm Andersson
A wonderful sweet man with heart of gold, just simply an awesome person!
That little house has just been given a permanent facelift
The anterior extension further up front creating a unique shift.
With its high ceiling made up of the finest quality of pine wood
This solid renovation is a beautiful structure that it just looks so good!
With an adult male buck lurking nearby in the thick bush
Many Norwegians have holiday homes that enjoy the serene hush.
I shall definitely visit the unique town of Tanumshede soon enough
And see that amazing Sunflower House that everybody knows and loves.

27.7.2014

Rising Star

Forty years ago, Malaysia gained independence and recited the patriotic oath
Already showing signs of pride, spotlighting the future's soaring growth.
Taking the first few steps like a baby learning how to walk
Malaysia has prospered into an economic force as great as a giant beanstalk.
Through the years, she has travelled a long and tedious distance
Foreseeing rough times ahead and gaining momentum with each distance.
It may have been a tough climb all the way up to reach the top
But Malaysia has never been a country to quit and just give up.
What she was then, compared to the beauty she is now
She can hold her head high for she has got a lot to show.
As the Petronas Twin towers erupts from the skyline of Kuala Lumpur
Standing out as the world tallest building with unique culture.
It boasts an economic boom sparked by foreign investments
In technology and manufacturing that is so advanced and intense.
It has made Malaysia one of the fastest developing countries in South East Asia
Stamping her mark on the world with her impeccable insignia.
The crowded streets reflect the country's mixed pallet of races
Ranging from Muslims, Christians, Buddhists, Sikhs and Hindus to the indigenous tribes.
Today, the 21 million people live in total peace and harmony
For, they can now go towards the new millennium with immense pride and dignity.

14.10.1997

Desolation

A lonely woman with a starving child
A sorry sight, yet tender and mild.
She sits at the entrance, stretching out her hand
Begging for someone to really understand.
But people just pass her by without a care
Talking jovially and pretending she isn't there.
How cruel and unkind can someone be
To ignore a need that is plain to see.
For day and night, she slaves to survive
To support her child; fighting for their lives.
Shunning them is a crime against humanity
Imagine, if it ever happened to you or me.
All she wants is a drop of kindness
Even ten paisa will bring her some happiness.
Seeing her child with an uncertain future
Is like an open wound without a suture.
Once rubbed with salt, it hurts like hell
For lonely twosome know this feeling only too well.
So, have a good heart along with a gentle smile
And give them some love & hope, even if it's just for a while.

8.12.1993

Monsoon Vengeance

It's hard to believe that just a few days ago
The days were hot and sultry, with no place to go.
Suddenly, things took turn for the better
Not caring how it happened, to bring us all together.
The clear sunny days transformed into gloomy skies
The dark angry clouds reflecting the storm in our eyes.
Our hearts beating like thunder rumbling through the night
As we watch lightning streak across the sky in fearsome delight.
Then, God unleashed his powerful fury held in a tight rein
And down it came in all its glory, the great torrential rain.
As it continued to pour like cats and dogs
Our friendship grew, finding a clear path through the fog.
Because of one person's malady responding to our caring nature
Our hearts, minds and souls united, slowly gaining stature.
Who could ever believe that such a thing would ever happen
The joy and love of our friendship that even rain could not dampen.
The closeness that we nurture will continue to grow and thrive
Imprinting every moment as a prominent mark in our lives.
Creating a distinct sweet harmony like a potent fragrance
Reflecting our everlasting friendship, through the monsoon vengeance.

6.6.1994

Lingering Shadows

The past is one thing we cannot seem to change
It follows us like a shadow through the distant range.
From the times of Shakespeare right up to the present day
It lingers on within us as our varied moods sway.
No matter how hard one tried to avoid or dodge it
It still manages to creep upon you within the limit.
Whatever we have done, whether it is good or really bad
Are all part of that shadow that makes us happy or sad.
Whatever sins we have committed cannot be undone
We just have to live with it and try to carry on.
Everyone has deep dark secrets kept hidden for so long
Suddenly it is out in the open, making everything go wrong.
Like a lingering shadow, the past refuses to set us free
Giving us a strong reminder of how things seem to be.
We may ask for forgiveness by giving confession in church
Knowing God will never leave us so abruptly, in a lurch.
Despite all the reasoning and thrashing out our doubts
One can never escape the past and figure a way out.
So, the only thing to do is to hope and pray for a new tomorrow
And create more happy and prosperous lingering shadows.

7.11.1994

Special Child

When you were born all those years ago
A beautiful baby your mom was proud to show.
With sparkling dark eyes, and a head full of hair
You were always restless, running here and there.
From the time you took your first step, you were hyperactive
Your childlike curiosity making you a super detective!
Faster than the speed of light, you grew up so fast
The metamorphosis that took place right from the past.
You have turned out to be a unique young woman
With a heart of gold, making you more human.
Your gentle smile giving encouragement to others
Your patience obstructing those who ruffle your feathers!
Your spontaneity and chronic sense of humour
Relieves even the stress of a very painful tumour!
But seriously though, you are truly one of a kind
There is no one like you in heart and in mind.
Whatever in life you choose to do, you will succeed
Because you are a friend in need who is a friend indeed!
Thanks to the special loving friendship that we share
Remember for you, I am always there.

23.11.1994

Survival

Life is too short to be taken seriously
Anything can happen at anytime to you or me.
Do not take everything for granted all the time
Every moment is worth than just a dime.
People come and go their own distant way
We make mistakes and utter words never to be said.
We always fool around and take things too easily
Not realizing that this world is as difficult as it can be.
Everyday is an intense struggle just to survive
Everybody is fighting for justice in their lives.
You get many shots and chances just to succeed
But you have only got one shot at yourself, indeed.
Nobody is a saint or an angel, today or tomorrow
Everyone will do anything – beg, steal or borrow.
To get what they want to achieve to be the best
To see who they can really trust is the ultimate test.
So one has to be cunning, shrewd and selfish these days
To get to the top by struggling up the winding staircase.
The lessons learned from the past long before
Will make us stronger survivors and wiser all the more.

3.12.1994

Far And Away

From far and away the cold winds blow
Heading swiftly towards the summer glow.
Reflecting the storm churning in our hearts
Finding its way like a ship on a chart.
From the distance, thunder rumbles through the sky
Gathering dark clouds which are present so high.
The waves come crashing so mightily to shore
So brilliant and beautiful, creating an uproar.
The sand, so coarse or fine, is totally pure
Caressed by the sea, making the land so secure.
The leaves of the trees rustle in the summer breeze
Comforting a troubled soul, putting his mind at ease.
For 'tis to the ocean we go, to seek silence and solace
The one and only quiet and solitary place.
Where we can set our minds completely free
And let go of our emotions where no one can see.
Oh! How wonderful it feels to cleanse the soul
To be one with nature and the sun's hues of gold.
For 'tis to the ocean we go, to fly far and away
To fulfill our dreams that we created yesterday.

16.11.1994

Stress Of The Press

When God created the world and the whole of mankind
He made it in such a way that found all of us in a bind
With all sorts of ingredients, he tossed up a great salad
Full of good, ugly, humour, sorrow, and of course, the bad.
As a student, I used to often wonder about all of these
Only one word comes to mind that does not seem to please.
It always gives me the hives, a headache and forces me to cram
Yikes! There comes that horrible word again – EXAM!
The punishing pace that we have to go through just to pass
Makes me wonder if it is really worth to bother with all the fuss.
Some of us work so hard and are still ever full of doubts
While others are just so damned lucky to have the easy way out.
There are moments like now, where I feel like I am about to explode
With my brains melting and hurting, my skull about to erode.
The amount of weight that I have lost, amounts to cachexia
All because of this draining exams that is slowly leading me to
dementia!
All I can say is that there is only one saving grace left for me
That is really God sent, making me slowly become tension free.
By having my sweet Mother with me is a blessing from heaven
As she gives me all the love and support to help me fulfill my ambition.

4.8.1995

Secret Realm

Morning shines pearly light on mist blanketing the rain forest
This lush wilderness portraying life at its very best.
Each leaf on every single tree is like a drama unfolding
A common agamid lizard stands statue still to catch a meal on the wing.
The myriad forms of life reveal their many hidden secrets
Creating a fragile and delicate refuge on a very much-crowded earth.
Two hundred feet off the ground, exotic treetops laced with vines
Create a canopy of infinite shades of colours so utterly divine.
The air within the forests is laden heavy with heat and humidity
Its lush greens lending a contrasting blend of coolness and serenity.
One crucial change in the forest's complex web of existence
Would alter even the survival of the pitcher plant, which is always uncertain.
A deadly monarsh moves through ground and water, shrouded in mystery
Elusive by nature, the cobra silently stalks its prey with a poison so deadly.
The rein of nature's age-old rhythm continues to this day
Like a grand master conducting the rehearsals of his play.
In this realm of eat and be eaten, puts every life form to the test
It will always boil down to the survival of the fittest.
Every day, we see plants and animals, some unnamed but still they parade
Such irreplaceable riches are surely worth saving, even as development speeds ahead.

14.10.1997

Beirut Rising

Known to the world as the Brick of the East
Where, many holidaymakers come to explore and have a feast.
Ruled by Syria and currently at war with Israel
Seeking a national identity that seems far from being cruel.
Tangled up in a web due to the ongoing war's causes
Battle lines have yielded to tan lines with roses.
Peace and a drive to prosper now seek to unite many former foes
In efforts to rebuild a country where humanity must fit the right shoes.
Ravaged buildings march like wounded soldiers along Beirut's Greenline
A defector boundary between the warring east and west ticking with time.
The immense struggle to overcome adversity caused by man and nature
Will take the patience of a saint to go through such extreme measures.
All Lebanese share a common goal and destiny of love and hope
Waiting in vain for something good like on a highly-strung rope.
Where peace is a mixture of coercion, encouragement and resolve
That, if provoked, could snap like a twig and dissolve.
Having to face a shaky economy, social inequities and regional unrest
Beirut will need all its resolve to sustain a lasting peace at its best.
But each day is full of uncertainty of the known leading into the unknown
As the truth unfolds, the winds of change will blow in the right direction.

22.11.1997

Nine Months

The origin of the child is that of the mother
A bond so strong that it is like no other.
From the time of conception, the meaning of life arose
The mother having hope and a good reason to rejoice.
Despite the hardships that will occur during the next 40 weeks
She will endure them, and a healthy baby she will seek.
As the days go by, the tiny zygote becomes an embryo
The gender of the unborn child still we do not know.
The embryo thus forms what will eventually be the foetus
This marvelous change will be a source of wonder to each one of us.
Months then go by and the child continues to grow inside
The baby's first kick, swelling even more its mother's love and pride.
Still she wonders if it will be an adorable little boy or a sweet little girl
Will the child's hair be straight or will it have a little curl?
The curiosities will keep on building till the very last moment
Until the time when the labour pains start, and her water bag has broken.
To her pleasant surprise, she has the healthiest set of twins
A little boy and a little girl, who has everyone tickled pink!
She now has something precious that no one can take away
Her unconditional love for her two children, who will live to see each day.

6.8.1996

Rememberance

Just the other day, I had some free time on my hands
Walking along the beach, my feet slipping through the sands.
Looking back at yesterday, reflecting on the years gone by
Remembering all the sweet hellos, and every sad goodbye.
I remember how very young and innocent we used to be
When we did not have any responsibilities and were always so carefree.
The days where we used to play, and laugh with utter joy
No jealousy between us when either of us received a brand new toy.
Through grade school, our friendship grew and became stronger
Even through all the jokes and bullying, we both stuck together.
As we matured into teenagers and entered into high school,
We became the best of friends who could outdo any other fool!
Our crazy escapades even then still bring a smile to my face
As I recollect our outrageous adventures in so many different places.
But just the thought of you is enough to make my day brighter
To chase my worries away and make my heart feel lighter.
It never ceases to amaze me that our friendship is over twenty years old
A friendship so precious and priceless as pure gold.
What would I be, if it were not for your soul reflected in me
Something I will always ponder as I gaze at the horizon beyond the sea.

7.8.1996

Into The Light

She thought she would never see the end of the tunnel
It was like squeezing through a narrow funnel.
The accident happened out of the blue
Making every memory become a hazy hue.
The frustration of having to cope with the after effects
To withhold her pride and to live with her defects.
She had the stamina and the intense grit
She took a lot of insults and a lot of dirt.
But she gave back as good as she took
Never letting the bullies off the sharp hook.
She could never walk for ten long agonising months
The pain and suffering, of which, she took the brunt.
But with the love and support of her family
She recovered well and happy for all to see.
Who said that there was anything impossible?
To her, anything and everything was possible.
For into the light she came at the end of the tunnel
Wrapped with love and confidence, the whole bundle.
For never again to let such a disaster strike
She is all set to conquer the world again, with a great hike.

29.12.1995

Unlawful Entry

A woman alone these days is a dangerous thing
All a guy is looking for is just a brief fling.
She puts all her love and trust in him
Giving herself with everything she has within.
Her devotion, her trust, her unconditional love
Like the very pureness of a light white dove.
For what seemed like forever, things were fine
Painted rosy red, so utterly true and divine.
Then arrived the unholiest of dark nights
Blinding her vision totally from the light.
As he dragged her into a blind alley after a date
Tearing at her clothes with pure hate.
His dark eyes blazing with fury and malice
His dislike for women taken out on the woman named Alice.
As he gained access for his unlawful entry
He tore apart her pride, her belief and her dignity.
When he was through with her, he left her to die
Fulfilling his lust, living to tell a lie.
By God's grace, she recovered slowly some months after
But his day of reckoning will definitely arrive sooner than later.

29.12.1995

Believe In Yourself

There are days when everything seems to go wrong
Nothing seems right and you are singing a sad song.
Everyone will surely ask you what the matter is
You will say, "It's nothing", and carry on like this.
Your insecurities firmly planted in your soul
Suppressing your feelings, the likes of tarnished gold.
You know deep down that you can do it if you try
But your fear of falling down makes you want to cry.
Life is full of battles, which cannot go away
Regardless of which direction the trees are going to sway.
Even though the greater man might always win
But the lesser man has always the greater strength within
Failure is always the ultimate pillar to success
The end result will always be victory and happiness.
The climb is always difficult up a steep ladder
But is definitely worth the challenge if you try harder.
Cultivate your imagination and put your mind to the test
Concentrate on big things and God will take care of the rest.
Believe in yourself and in everything that you do
In the end, all your dreams and aspirations will come true.

10.11.1995

Totally Sane, Totally Crazy

I came to KMC thinking I knew everything
With my father in tow and my hand in a sling.
Took one look at my medical college painted in ghastly green
It was one of the ugliest buildings that we had ever seen!
My life began as a freshman that was scared to bits
With all the seniors lurking about, showing off their teeth.
The torture of ragging that poor me had to endure
From the hostel to the college bank, and classes galore.
The humiliating things that we were all made to do
Were really harmless, and also kind of funny too.
Imagine standing on a chair, and singing the Indian national anthem
Poking fun at your hair, and commenting on each strand of them!
The years progressed to a point when I became a sophomore
With a new batch of "freshies" not like the ones before.
Some strutted their stuff as if they had been to exotic places
While others had horrified expressions on their faces!
Now as a full-fledged senior, I can do as I please
With a newfound confidence and courage that I can carry with ease.
For I came to KMC totally sane and really happy
And I shall leave this place in one piece and totally crazy!

10.11.1995

Cycle Of Death

The crushed body of a Tutsi boy
Lying in a lonesome church long destroyed.
Amidst the genocidal spasm taking place
The poor soul lost his head along with his face.
The cycle of death continues its blemished course
The world chaotic as the international community recoils.
Bodies of children lined up for mass burials
Unable to be identified by their own familial.
Will the murderous spree in Rwanda ever end?
Will there ever be hope just around the bend?
The presence of peacekeepers doesn't do much good
It's like the Merry Men without Robin Hood!
The slaughter continues everyday with a vengeance
With respective tribes pledging their allegiance.
No food, no water, no latrines available
No wonder this Earth is never amiable!
The Government turns their guns on the innocent victims
And they said justice prevails for all times!
So, I ask you time and time again, my dear friend
Will the murder and genocide in Rwanda ever end?

20.12.1995

The Citadel

Talk about sexual discrimination at large
The male species think that they are the greatest to emerge.
Sorry to disappoint you, oh mighty men
But here to stay are the stronger women.
What happened to the female recruit at the Citadel
Is one story everyone will always remember well.
She fought and lost a worthy cause
Creating a controversy that has made us pause.
To think and rethink about male chauvinism
Bringing men to use their brains and face realism.
That the Citadel ought to break their 152 year-old-history
And learn to accept women in uniform more freely.
The death threats she received were most unkind
Putting more pressure on her, leaving her in a bind.
But she walked out with her head held high
Her sense of pride still intact as time passed her by.
To all the men in this glorious era today
Stop what you are doing and hear what I have to say.
You are now an equal to us great women
And you shall live with this lesson and truly learn.

9.12.1995

Is There A God?

Some beliefs are so strong that they just overwhelm and consume you
Then you hear so many different things that you do not know what to do.
The faith that has been passed down through generations
Seems so firmly embedded in a mind full of confusion.
Is there a God who praises peace and beauty?
Is Satan hovering at the edge, playing with our sanity?
Who is right or wrong is not the question here
It is whether we want to really believe and desire.
There are some moments like now where I ponder
Are my prayers being answered as I try harder?
Is the fear that I feel for the unknown natural?
Or is it a myth that people have made real?
Such milestones have been achieved since the days of Jesus
Through all the wars that tore this planet to pieces.
Yet, there is a God who put things back together
And let us live our lives for worse or for better.
Is what I practice always at par with what I preach?
Will I find the truth until the end of my search?
The restlessness in me will always prode me on
Till the day I reach heaven, when the Earth is gone.

14.12.1995

Cheers And Tears

There are happy moments along with the blues
One time we are flying high, and then we are out of tune.
The pressures build gradually as the day wanes
The sunlight is fading; it is glinting off the windowpanes.
Everyday begins with a brand new ray of hope
Promises reflected in my book and stethoscope.
My victories have been momentous and joyful
The disappointments have been totally dreadful.
Despite the cheers which follow my success
The underlying sadness will always hide my tears.
No matter how hard I try to be cheerful
The loner in me will always be fearful.
About what the next day holds in store
Makes me more anxious than ever before.
The sudden insecurities all come crashing down
In an instant there is total chaos all around.
Good times are short-lived compared to the bad
Makes you wish that it would last longer just a tad.
But there is something that I have learnt from my peers
That life is certainly full of cheers and tears.

9.12.1995

A Nation's Conecscience

A soldier's confession breaks open the damn
Telling everything about the atrocities done by man.
From the killing of Egyptian POWs by the Isrealis
It was all over in just a couple of minutes.
But actually, it is not over just as yet
The tempest has just begun to actually set.
The slaughter in the Sinai was just the beginning of many
Transcending down to the present day as seen so clearly.
What are we doing and what have we become?
Do not we realise that these people too have homes?
Who gives a damn what religion they are
So what if they are Muslims and Jews by far?
We are all responsible for our individual actions
For the dead and the living, we show our compassion.
These innocent soldiers did not deserve to die
All these years, the whole cover-up was just a big lie.
But now that the truth has all but come out
The assassins shall pay the price without a doubt.
May the souls of the victims rest in peace
For justice shall prevail and set our minds at ease.

9.12.1995

The Bosnian Bombardment

Everyone deserves a fair chance in his or her lives
From the young to the aged, from the men to their wives.
But luck seems to have run out on them
Their race and religion, the Serbs seem to condemn.
Which creased face of age will tell the true story?
Which howl from a lonely child shall set her free?
The whole nation is choking itself towards extinction
The whole system needs to make a firm decision.
Why is mankind so cruel to his brotherhood?
For all these people form the universality of victimhood.
This whole nonsense of ethnic cleansing is all bullshit
Killing innocent people and dumping them in huge pits.
What do the Serbs gain by promoting such atrocities?
Ignoring the growing number of casualties.
What difference does it really make who we really are
We are only human whether from near or afar.
Based on vengeful mythologies and minor cultural differences
The Serbs intend to wipe out the entire Muslim circumference.
The sins they have committed shall reflect upon their fate one day
It is all in God's hands as He will make sure of the dear price they will
have to pay.

8.12.1995

20th Century Blues

Stress, anxiety, depression – all rolled into one
The current trend carried by almost everyone.
Careers seem to come first before families
To the point of being obsessive and going crazy!
The race to be the best seem to consume man
Like Westerners trying so hard to obtain a tan!
With the environment just going down the drain
The fog and the pollution preventing the falling rain.
The hole in the Ozone slowly becoming the size of Europe
Making breathing more difficult as we climb the slope.
With the modernisation of technology so advanced
How do we cope with the excessive load or demand.
Man can only do so much with just a pair of hands
Why can't we just simply and easily understand?
That we are just pushing ourselves beyond the limit
Just what are we trying to prove, and whom are we trying to beat?
The roots of modern maladies lie in our genes
Descending from past generations now to be seen.
All of these discovered through evolutionary psychology
What the future holds for us, we just have to wait and see.

8.12.1995

Something To Remember

Once burnt, twice shy as the saying goes
At the final breakup, you are full of woes
You had all your hopes up all this time
But she broke your heart without reason or rhyme.
The promises she made to you all seem empty now
The love she gave to you has all disappeared somehow.
There is a big void inside that echoes your sorrow
Hoping and praying for a brand new tomorrow.
The conflicts and disagreements were always there
Both sets of parents were totally against the whole affair.
Despite all the odds, you gave it your all
But in the end, you really did have a great fall.
Even after parting and agreeing to stay as friends
You are still in a bind and crossed at the bend.
Your wounds are still fresh as it was yesterday
But they will heal in time, come what may.
You have friends around you that really care
The deep love, support and friendship that we all share.
There are plenty of fish out there in the sea
Just be your wonderful self, always happy and carefree.

6.12.1995

The Baltimore Connection

Dedicated to my dear best friend, Bobby Vijay.

Some people say that you are a royal flirt
While others used to say that you are not as nice as your shirt.
But I know you well enough to know by now
That rumours just fly about somehow.
You are like a rare precious stone inside
Your honesty shines through on the side.
When you love, you give yourself completely
Your mind, body and soul living peacefully.
Your depth and sensitivity for others is so pure
Your presence in our lives is like a soothing cure.
Even in your dilemma, you make others laugh
You take things so easy even when the going gets tough.
You can really be stubborn as a proverbial mule
Your pride so strong to withstand the pull.
Your protectiveness and loyalty towards your friends
Surround us like a loving cloud till no end.
You have always been there through thick and thin
You are a fighter, for somehow you will always win.
Always remember the good times that we share
As one of your best friends, for you, I shall always be there.

6.12.1995

Love And Care For Old Parents

Written by my wonderful mother, Arati Bardhan.

From the day we are born
Our parents toil, bringing us up with great care
To become good, responsible, well-mannered adults
Sacrifice and endure all obstacles they lovingly bear.

Good values and discipline well taught and instilled
Without any thought of hardship and neglect.
Train children to be humble, honest and obedient
Gradually developing them to feel secure and great.

As parents grow weak and older
They are left to fend themselves all alone
To cope life with indignity and no mental support
Leaving them with their hearts all torn.

As children grow into adulthood and start life
Gradually forget the solidly built attachment
A bond that was very strong and graceful before
Showing only qualities of selfishness and detachment.

Old Parents become insecure and helpless
Dejected, disappointed and totally unwanted.
Can't we prevent this undignified, incurable disease
Just with a spoon of love and care for them, to feel protected?

Is this what children do, without feeling any guilt
Neglect old parents and store them with sadness?
The younger generation watches and learns fast
Only to tear the strong family bond and develop selfishness.

Such horrible behavior isn't life's good progress
For it's only a part of the unavoidable bad education
When human reasoning power becomes absolutely void
One tends to forget good values without any hesitation!!

Until adulthood, family bond is always strong
Feeling proud, safe, steady and happy.
After marriage, relationships reverse tremendously
Drowning all the days of strong love and carefree.

In-Laws had been always a debatable issue
Coping with them is quite hard and trying!!
When patience, tolerance and loving care shown
Can change their negative behavior and dealings.

Till infinity, this malicious cycle will repeat
So let's change our mind set and bad feelings.
Shower old parents with love and care
Only two ingredients needed to get their Godly blessings.

Arati Bardhan

5th September 2013